LONDON'S ROYAL RIV

Michael St John Parker

Measured by the standards of the Amazon or the Nile, the Yangtze or the Danube, the Thames is a provincial stream of almost insignificant size; yet its history and its role in the life of the English nation entitle it to a place among the great rivers of the world, and it exerts a peculiar magic and power of its own, which have caused it to be a source of fascination and delight to countless generations. Whatever changes it may have seen and undergone, in one respect the Thames remains as it has been since the time of Alfred the Great — it is a royal river, strung with palaces like precious stones on a necklace and rich in majestic associations.

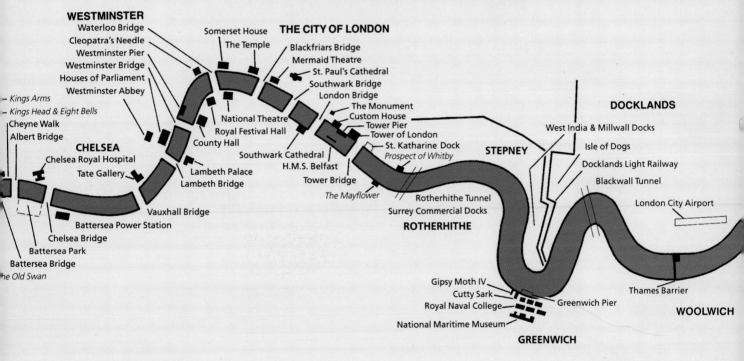

WESTMINSTER
- Waterloo Bridge
- Cleopatra's Needle
- Westminster Pier
- Westminster Bridge
- Houses of Parliament
- Westminster Abbey

Somerset House
The Temple

THE CITY OF LONDON
- Blackfriars Bridge
- Mermaid Theatre
- St. Paul's Cathedral
- Southwark Bridge
- London Bridge
- The Monument
- Custom House
- Tower Pier
- Tower of London
- St. Katharine Dock

Prospect of Whitby

DOCKLANDS
- West India & Millwall Docks
- Isle of Dogs
- Docklands Light Railway
- Blackwall Tunnel

London City Airport

STEPNEY

- *Kings Arms*
- *Kings Head & Eight Bells*
- Cheyne Walk
- Albert Bridge

CHELSEA
- Chelsea Royal Hospital
- Tate Gallery

National Theatre
Royal Festival Hall
County Hall
Southwark Cathedral
H.M.S. Belfast
Tower Bridge

Lambeth Palace
Lambeth Bridge

Vauxhall Bridge

Battersea Power Station
Chelsea Bridge
Battersea Park
Battersea Bridge
The Old Swan

The Mayflower

Rotherhithe Tunnel
Surrey Commercial Docks

ROTHERHITHE

Thames Barrier

Gipsy Moth IV
Cutty Sark
Royal Naval College
National Maritime Museum

Greenwich Pier

WOOLWICH

GREENWICH

LEFT: Windsor Castle from across the river. William the Conqueror first established a fort here in the 11th century, and the Castle has played a central role in British royal history ever since.

RIGHT: Eton College, one of Britain's most famous schools, founded by Henry VI in 1440.

FAR RIGHT: Runnymede. In 1215, not far from this spot, King John reluctantly agreed to a document, which became known as the Magna Carta, restricting his arbitrary powers and confirming the rights of free men under the law of the land.

RIGHT, BELOW: The House on the Bridge, a restaurant at Eton. There are many popular restaurants and public houses along the banks of the Thames.

To take a boat along the Thames is to follow in the wake of countless royal journeys, and where better to begin our voyage than at Windsor, beneath the frowning walls and lofty towers of one of the oldest and grandest of all the royal castles.

William the Conqueror first established a fortress here, on a bluff above the river plain, and nearly every monarch since then has added his or her contribution to make the castle stronger, or more splendid, or just more habitable. It is still a fortress, as guards in scarlet tunics and beetling bearskins bear imperturbable witness — and a shrine of medieval chivalry, too, with the chapel of the Order of the Garter in the outer ward. But it is also the principal seat of the Royal House of Windsor, to which, indeed, it has given its name.

The outline plan of the courtyards has not altered much since the 12th century, but the buildings themselves have been remodelled to meet the changing requirements of the Royal Family who, since George III, have taken a particular delight in Windsor Castle, favouring it as a private as well as a public

residence. Much work was done in the early 19th century by Sir Jeffry Wyatville, architect to George IV, who restored walls and towers dismantled in the time of Charles II, raised the Round Tower to its present commanding height, and remodelled the magnificent, treasure-crammed State Apartments. Queen Victoria, in her turn, spent money lavishly on Windsor, and the castle is steeped in associations with the Queen-Empress, who lies buried with her husband, Prince Albert, in Frogmore Mausoleum in the Home Park.

Many kings have hunted in these parklands (and not only kings, it seems, for it is said that the Great Park is haunted by the sinister, stag-headed apparition of Herne the Hunter, with his deadly hounds!), George III established a model farm here, and modern monarchs enjoy the pleasures of racing at Ascot in one of the most colourful weeks of the English social season.

Just across the river from Windsor is another royal foundation of legendary splendour — Eton College, the charity school that became the nursery of a ruling class. Five patrician centuries have endowed it with a uniquely rich and brilliant history, so that its very stones seem to speak of prime ministers and poets, generals and judges, the rich, the brilliant and the powerful, who have spent their schooldays there. It is a curiously open place, however, in feeling at least; some schools turn their backs monastically on the world, others confront it with severe and threatening disapproval, but Eton waits with serene assurance for the world to come a-courting.

Chertsey, Shepperton (of film studios fame) and Molesey bring us to the next of the great palaces which line the banks of the lower Thames: Hampton Court, often regarded as the richest, and certainly the largest, of English royal residences. It was first built by Cardinal Wolsey, whose power and pride were stunningly demonstrated by its thousand rooms, large and small, with their sumptuous decorations. Such opulence attracted the envy and eventually the distrust of King Henry VIII, and Wolsey felt obliged to present his palace to the Crown in 1525. The royal extortioner spent more than one of his honeymoons there; the future Edward VI was born there at the cost of his mother's life; and there Catherine Howard was arrested — her ghost is said to haunt the Long Gallery, still screaming for mercy.

William III, 150 years after these Tudor melodramas were played, commissioned Sir Christopher Wren to carry out an extensive remodelling of the palace. The resulting State Apartments and gardens, together with the spreading grounds themselves — a remarkable survival of late 17th-century landscape gardening — stand among Wren's greatest achievements. Their staid, almost homely dignity can be set in sharp, fascinating contrast with the coldly absolutist arrogance of Louis XIV's Versailles, which was being built at the same time.

No monarch has lived at Hampton Court since George II. George III is said to have conceived a dislike for the place when a boy, as a result of having his ears publicly boxed by his grandfather one day in the State Apartments. For generations now the palace, with its priceless treasures, has been open to the public as part of the national heritage.

Beyond Hampton Court the river curves northwards to Kingston-on-Thames, which boasts ancient associations with royalty. It was the coronation place of 10th-century Saxon kings, and their Coronation Stone is preserved there still.

ABOVE: A view of Hampton Court Palace from the river. The last monarch to live here was George II, and today it houses a magnificent collection of paintings, furniture and tapestries.

RIGHT: A tranquil scene at Hampton, where sailing is a favourite pastime.

ABOVE: Teddington Lock, the largest of 44 locks and weirs along the length of the river.

BELOW: Marble Hill House with its beautifully laid out grounds. It was built in the Palladian style for a mistress of George II.

At Teddington Lock, below Kingston, the Thames becomes a tidal stream, and from this point the river is controlled by the Port of London Authority. Vulgar commerce still seems far removed from this elegant reach of the river, however, where the thronging suburbs seem to hang respectfully back from the banks lined with the stately mansions of 17th- and 18th-century aristocrats. Richmond and Twickenham, on opposite banks of the river, were much patronised by leaders of society from the late 17th century onwards — the politicians, the wits, the bright stars of fashion. Some of their houses still remain: Ham House, on the Richmond side, retains remarkable examples of Stuart decor and furnishings, while opposite in Twickenham is the Orleans House Gallery, built by James Gibbs in 1720, and the haughty elegance of Marble Hill House, created for a mistress of George II. Alexander Pope lived at Twickenham, and a relic of his elaborate gardens remains in the form of a mutilated but still curious 'grotto'. A more important, and complete, survival of 18th-century dilettantism is Horace Walpole's fantasy house, Strawberry Hill, also at Twickenham; here, some would say, is the fountain-head of the movement known as the Gothic Revival.

More varied — and vulgar — associations cluster around Eel-Pie Island; Henry VIII stopped his barge there to enjoy the delicacy which gave the place its name, wealthy Edwardians threw notoriously extravagant parties in the hotel there, and the Rolling Stones performed in a 1960s nightclub. But on the firmer ground of the river banks we are back with royal palaces and stately memories.

Richmond is a royal manor of almost immemorial antiquity, and the palace which once stood there was a favourite residence of Plantagenet and Tudor rulers. Edward III died here, and so, amid death-bed drama and intrigue, did Elizabeth I. In lighter vein, the charming traditional air 'On Richmond Hill' still carries echoes of the philandering pursuits of the Prince Regent in the early years of the 19th century, when the view from Richmond Hill seems, if we can trust the painted

ABOVE: The Thames at Richmond is a popular subject with local artists.

LEFT: Ham House, built in 1610. It is now owned by the National Trust and contains many treasures from the Victoria and Albert Museum.

RIGHT: The well-loved view of the river from Richmond Hill.

BELOW: Syon House. The interior reveals some of the finest examples of Robert Adam's work, and the grounds were laid out by Capability Brown.

record, to have been as idyllic as any in England. White Lodge in Richmond Park, now occupied by the Royal Ballet School, saw the birth of the future King Edward VIII in 1894.

Richmond itself is plainly a village that has grown into a suburban town, with its green still ringed with enviably elegant houses. Hardly less notable, though, is the splendid array of buildings which confronts the river at the south end of Richmond Bridge — unquestionably the grandest, most whole-hearted and convincing exercise in the classical manner to have been executed in Britain since the war. The architect was Quinlan Terry.

Across the river in Twickenham the stands of the famous Rugby Union Football Ground tower over the suburban houses. London's (and England's) rugby enthusiasts throng here to cheer on their teams in the fiercely fought international and other major matches played through the winter months.

ABOVE: Kew Palace was built in the Dutch style for a London merchant in 1631. George III loved this house and lived in it for many years.

RIGHT: The Chinese Pagoda in Kew Gardens. The 300 acres provide a haven of peace but are also used for serious botanical research.

Aristocratic opulence is not left behind at Richmond; if anything, indeed, we move into an area of still greater splendour as we approach Kew and Chiswick.

Isleworth, on the north bank, still boasts some fine 17th- and 18th-century mansions, and a pillared boathouse attributed to the landscape architect Capability Brown; but this stretch of the river is dominated by the ducal grandeurs of Syon House, London residence of the Percys, dukes of Northumberland, who made it a centre for political plots and intrigues in Tudor and Stuart times. Named after the monastery founded on the site in 1415 by King Henry V, the house was reshaped in palatial style from 1762 onwards by Robert Adam; in the Great Hall and Ante-Room, in particular, he achieved some of his most sublime effects — as Sir John Betjeman once said on a television programme, 'you'd never guess that battlemented house contained such wonders as there are inside it'. The grounds (which now contain a garden centre) were laid out by Capability Brown.

'Look on this house, it is a joy in stone
And many woods, wrought by
ingenious men,
Not for the edge of time,
But for futurity.'
ADRIAN BURY

Practically opposite Syon Park are the Royal Botanic Gardens at Kew, a world-famous centre of scientific botany. Its 300 acres of gardens form one of the most beautiful pleasure-grounds in all England, especially when daffodils, bluebells or rhododendrons are in bloom. Some 45,000 species of plants grow in the gardens, and over 7,000,000 dried specimens are preserved in the Herbarium. The gardens were founded in 1759 by Princess Augusta, mother of George III; it was at her behest that Sir William Chambers built the delightful, 163 feet high Chinese Pagoda. George III was particularly fond of the charming 17th-century, Dutch-style house known as Kew Palace, and many souvenirs of this much misunderstood monarch are to be found there.

From Kew to Chiswick Mall past Strand-on-the-Green the waterfronts are adorned by elegant houses. Pride of them all is Chiswick House, an exquisite Palladian villa begun in 1725 to the designs of the connoisseur Lord Burlington, assisted by William Kent; both men lie buried in St Nicholas' church nearby.

ABOVE: Some pretty riverside dwellings at Strand-on-the-Green, many of which date from the 18th century.

It is perhaps one of the most aristocratic buildings ever erected in England, and its quality has survived even the attentions of modern government ministries, who sometimes seem to have been unwisely inspired by Pope's famous lines on Chiswick:

'Erect new wonders and the old repair;
Jones and Palladio to themselves restore
And be whate'er Vitruvius was before.'

OF THE USE OF RICHES

RIGHT: The elegant Italian-inspired Chiswick House, built in 1730.

For a century after its completion the rich, the clever and the powerful thronged here.

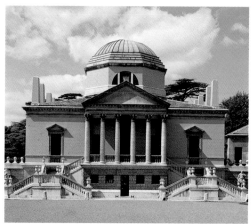

LEFT: Hammersmith Bridge, completed in 1887.

BELOW LEFT: Battersea Power station, built in the early 1930s by Sir George Gilbert Scott, the famous ecclesiastical architect. No longer used as a power station, it is to become a huge family leisure centre.

The great double curve of the Thames below Chiswick is nowadays more famous for oarsmen than for aristocrats; Mortlake and Hammersmith, Barnes and Putney, are names made famous by Oxford and Cambridge Boat Race commentaries, and the boathouses of London rowing clubs line the south bank towards Fulham.

Fulham itself is an ugly district adorned by a famous and popular football club; Hurlingham House, now an exclusive club and formerly a famous polo ground; and Fulham Palace, the venerable residence of the bishops of London, with 1,200 years of uninterrupted ecclesiastical history.

The south bank of the river from this point onwards is grimly and determinedly industrial. The most striking landmark of the reach is Battersea power station; at the time of its building, in the 1930s, it was seen as a triumph of progress, a monument to the idealism of 'modern planning'; now it has outlived its original use. There is a £50 million plan afoot which is destined to turn the power station into an enormous indoor

ABOVE: Albert Bridge, at Chelsea, named after Queen Victoria's dearly-loved consort, was opened in 1873.

ABOVE LEFT:
The Hammersmith Bridge coat of arms.

LEFT: A houseboat on the embankment at Chelsea.

leisure centre designed to overcome the vagaries of the British weather. The Victorian cast-iron elegance of Albert Bridge, on the other hand, wears well, and the vista of this happily ornamental structure, festive with lights and colour, cheers the mind like champagne.

Chelsea, on the north bank, offers a fascinating contrast to Battersea. From the 16th century, when Sir Thomas More had a mansion by the riverside here, Chelsea has combined the character of a fashionable suburb with that of an intellectual and artistic Latin quarter; its style and verve make it one of the most distinctive of London's 'villages'. Fielding, Smollett, Turner, Mrs Gaskell, Carlyle, George Eliot, Rossetti, Swinburne, Whistler, Oscar Wilde, Sargent, Wilson Steer, Augustus John, Lloyd George are only some of the famous names associated with Chelsea. Several of these

people lived in the row of waterfront houses known as Cheyne Walk.

Easily the most distinguished building to be seen along the Chelsea Embankment is the Royal Hospital, founded by Charles II in 1682 for the support of army veterans, and designed by Sir Christopher Wren. Its three splendid quadrangles, parts of which are open to the public, and the 500 picturesquely dressed In-Pensioners, are famous tourist attractions; but they are also part of a proudly living military tradition.

More modern, and no less assertive than the Royal Hospital, are the Tate Gallery and the Vickers Building which mark the way to Westminster. The former, named after its founding benefactor, the sugar-refiner Sir Henry Tate, houses one of the nation's greatest collections of art, including contemporary works.

LEFT: Lambeth Palace, the London seat of the archbishops of Canterbury since the 13th century. The Lollards' Tower is a memorial to John Wyclif, religious reformer, who was tried here in 1378. The Great Hall was built in the 17th century. In 1787 the first American bishops were consecrated here.

RIGHT: The Houses of Parliament by night. Still known as the Palace of Westminster, it was a royal residence from the 11th to the 16th centuries. The fire of 1834 destroyed everything except Westminster Hall, which dates from 1097, part of St Stephen's Chapel and Edward III's little Jewel Tower.

From the tall Vickers tower onwards, the scale of the waterfront changes; now we are in the heart of the capital, and passing the headquarters of its political and commercial activity. On the left are the spires and pinnacles of Westminster, on the right the tree-bowered battlements of Lambeth Palace testify to the ancient English alliance of Church and State. Discreetly separated by the width of the Thames from the royal seat of Westminster, Lambeth has been the London residence of the archbishops of Canterbury since the 13th century. Today, in addition, it is the administrative centre of the world-wide Anglican Communion. Among other treasures housed within its walls, the library of some 100,000 volumes is especially important to bibliophiles and historians.

For most visitors, however, the dominant attraction along this reach of the river must be the Palace and Abbey of Westminster, both of them founded by Edward the Confessor. For five centuries a strongpoint of royal power, the palace is nowadays identified with representative government and parliamentary democracy. The present Houses of Parliament were designed by Sir Charles Barry, following a disastrous fire in 1834, and the buildings, which include the famous Clock Tower housing Big Ben, were completed in 1860 when the Victoria Tower, nearly 400 feet high, was finished. The only major parts of the old royal residence to have survived are the Great Hall, built by William II between 1097 and 1099, with its magnificent hammer-beam roof dating from the reign of Richard II, and the crypt and cloister of St Stephen's Chapel.

The Palace of Westminster as we see it today is a vast building; it covers eight acres, has eleven courtyards, and two miles of passages, and contains over 1,000 rooms. It is a complete little town in itself — and it is said that not even the most knowledgeable of its inhabitants knows all the secrets of its gigantic fabric.

The State Opening of Parliament, at the start of a new parliamentary session in the autumn of each year, or after a General Election, sees the Palace of Westminster in its

ABOVE: Sir Charles Barry designed the present Houses of Parliament in the mid-19th century. They have recently been cleaned and restored to their original glorious colour.

most public and stately mood. Amid glittering ceremonial and to the sound of trumpets, the Queen takes her seat on the throne of the House of Lords, and calls to her presence the members of the House of Commons, to hear the Government's proposals for the forthcoming legislation. The whole occasion provides a public summary of the history of the British institution of constitutional monarchy. Needless to say, everyday life in Parliament is more sober, but it is no less fascinating, whether you consider it as mere spectacle, or as the reality of representative government in operation.

Still more of a national shrine, in every sense, is Westminster Abbey. English kings and queens have been crowned here since the time of William the Conqueror; its vaults are crowded with the tombs and its walls with the memorials of the good, the great and the famous, from saints and poets to generals and politicians; and the countless treasures of art and history which enrich its soaring Gothic beauties make it in all respects a jewel-house of the nation's heritage. Much of the fabric dates from the 14th and 15th centuries, but the western towers, which give the great church an outline perhaps as well known as any in Europe, were not added until 1734.

13

The Thames from Westminster to Tower Bridge presents perhaps its most familiar — but also its most majestic — face. Immediately below Westminster Bridge it is closely lined with the massive buildings of central government. For sheer pretentiousness, however, even they cannot rival the gigantically ponderous facade of County Hall, or the wind-battered, Orwellian boxes of the Shell Building, both on the South Bank. When the tide is low, and mudflats glisten slimily beneath the rattling girders of Charing Cross railway bridge, we see with a vengeance the river's grimly urban aspect, the inspiration of painters such as Monet and Whistler. Here, as elswhere, grey is a tone which seems natural to the South Bank, and it is dominant also in the concrete and glass of the clustered 'culture-palaces' which huddle together as if for mutual protection at the south end of Waterloo Bridge. The Royal Festival Hall and National Film Theatre date from 1951; other buildings, including two more concert-halls, an art gallery, and a long-

ABOVE: Cleopatra's Needle, presented to Britain in 1819 by Mehemet Ali, viceroy of Egypt. Despite the name, it has no connection with Cleopatra.

LEFT, ABOVE: A view from the top of the Houses of Parliament towards County Hall.

LEFT, BELOW: Somerset House, which became well-known as the home of the Probate Registry. Recently its Fine Rooms have been restored for exhibitions.

ABOVE: Waterloo Bridge, with the modern City skyline and dome of St Paul's in the distance.

RIGHT: The National Theatre, opened in 1976, is part of the South Bank cultural area which includes the Festival Hall, the Hayward Gallery and the Museum of the Moving Image.

awaited National Theatre, have since been added. They are earnest-looking but they house music and drama which are the legitimate pride of London.

The north bank, by contrast, speaks here of high Victorian ostentation and endeavour. The broad, leafy boulevard of the Victoria Embankment, created between 1864 and 1870, with its floridly decorated lamps and ponderous stone parapets, runs from Westminster to Blackfriars, past a succession of floating piers and moored vessels. Among other monuments on the Embankment is the 68-feet high pink granite obelisk from Heliopolis known as Cleopatra's Needle; dating from *c.*1500 BC, it was presented to the British people in 1819, but reached its present site only after many adventures.

The area between the river and the Strand was for centuries dominated by great houses which are all now no more than names. Somerset House, however, was acquired by

the Crown in 1552, and rebuilt by Sir William Chambers between 1776 and 1786; today its coolly elegant façade adds distinction to the riverfront and rebukes the brashness of its neighbours. The 18th century holds sway also in the calm precinct of the Temple, further east, where spacious gardens lap round the rectilinear blocks of lawyers' chambers, austere in detail but imposing in composition, like some measured epitome of the legal ideal.

15

Beyond Blackfriars we become aware that we have left behind the political, legal, administrative and cultural part of the capital; now the tone is decidedly commercial, even though the ravages of German bombs and the movement of trade downstream have taken much of the life away from the old sea port. But first comes a stretch of river associated with a unique episode in the annals of the theatre, for it was on Bankside, a narrow strip of ground along the south bank where Londoners in Tudor times went to seek their pleasures, that the Elizabethan drama suddenly blossomed and flourished. The Globe Theatre, for which Shakespeare wrote his plays, vanished in the 17th century, but there is a project, set afoot by the American impresario and entrepreneur, Sam Wanamaker, to recreate it on a site close to the original. Most recently, archaeological discoveries made under the noses of developers near Southwark Bridge have revealed the actual timbers of a late Elizabethan theatre — the very boards, perhaps, trodden by Shakespeare and Marlowe. Less grand relics, but perhaps even more moving, are thousands of hazelnut shells, which litter the site of the theatre's pit — the nuts were the popcorn of Tudor playgoers!

One of the comparatively small number of historic buildings which still survive on the south bank, and one which has close connections with that early heroic period of the English theatre, is Southwark Cathedral, tucked away in a tranquil corner among railway viaducts and roaring lorries. One of the earliest and most distinguished settlers of North America, John Harvard, founder of the university which bears his name, was baptised here in 1607. He is commemorated today in the chapel of St John, specially restored as the Harvard Chapel by members of the university. Today the cathedral is prized as one of the finest Gothic buildings remaining in London, and imaginative redevelopment is creating around it a new townscape of courtyards and walkways which is attracting increasing numbers of visitors.

It needs a considerable effort of the imagination to envisage Elizabethan gallants, ruffed and rapiered, swaggering through Southwark; but around this stage of our river-voyage the eye is readily caught and the mind stirred by that symbol of a later London, the dome of St Paul's, riding poised yet massive above the rooftops of the City. Sir Christopher Wren's creation no longer presides in unrivalled majesty over a complementary townscape of baroque towers and steeples, as he designed it should in the 1670s; post-war skyscrapers, even more than Hitler's Blitz, have marred his conception of London's skyline as a harmonious symphony in stone. But the great church still flings its challenge to the clouds.

St Paul's has seen many royal occasions, notably Prince Charles's wedding, but it is much more a national than a royal temple. In times of peril and of triumph, the nation's leaders have joined in solemn prayer at St Paul's. It has watched the rise and fall of empire; its vaults have rung to Marlborough's Te Deums, Nelson is buried here, and Wellington, and at the end of the day the funeral trumpets sounded here beneath the dome for Winston Churchill, last and greatest of imperial statesmen.

Other historic associations than those of imperial grandeur may, however, be evoked by the sight of St Paul's dome. It is for many the characteristic symbol of that almost-vanished City of London, the living town depicted by a series of great writers from Chaucer through Pepys to Dickens. It was a city of winding alleyways and crowded streets, of grand livery halls cheek by jowl with desperate, teeming slums, of galleried inns and dusty warehouses, of smoke-blackened churches and grimy counting-houses. Above all it was a riverside city, and glimpses of it may still be seen from the river today, lurking at the feet of the wind-whipped office blocks which, like invading aliens, have caused the depopulation of the old town within living memory.

Ironically, it is the south bank, so long despised by the City grandees opposite, that now boasts some of the most imaginative and attractive architecture along this reach of the Thames. Recent years have seen a hectic redevelopment of areas devastated by the war and left derelict by the downstream movement of London's port business. Every style of building seems to be represented, often on a gigantic scale, and some of the most ambitious schemes, such as the Hay's Galleria, a shopping mall on the site of the old Hay's Wharf, are brilliantly light, with their cascades of glasswork, and dashingly styled — enormously exciting to look at and to walk in. And everywhere there are wine bars, thronged with City types from across the water — the south bank has indeed come up in the world!

RIGHT: Dawn breaks over the great dome of St Paul's.

INSET: Fireworks over St Paul's. The cathedral was built between 1675 and 1710 by Sir Christopher Wren after the Great Fire of London in 1666. It has a magnificent Renaissance exterior and the cross surmounting the dome stands 365 feet above the ground.

O ne of the newest things along this
reach of the river has the oldest name
– London Bridge. Here was a principal origin of the City's wealth and impor-
tance, marking as it did the upper limit of
navigation and the lowest crossing-point
before the sea. In fact, until the construction
of a bridge at Westminster in the 1740s, it had
no rival in the capital. 'Old London Bridge'
was built during the last quarter of the 12th
century and it carried a street of shops and
houses on its 19 narrow arches, much like the
Ponte Vecchio which still survives in
Florence. It was protected by two fortified
gates and broken by drawbridges, and was
graced by a chapel dedicated in honour of the
sainted Londoner Thomas Becket. Further
edification, of a grisly sort, was offered to
passengers in the shape of the mouldering
heads of decapitated traitors, which were
stuck on poles over the southern gatehouse.
This picturesque accumulation survived until
1756, when the buildings were cleared away,

LEFT, ABOVE: Aerial view showing Tower Bridge and HMS *Belfast*.

LEFT, BELOW: The River Thames from Tower Bridge. The cruiser HMS *Belfast*, a veteran of the Second World War, is now permanently berthed in the Pool of London as part of the Imperial War Museum.

ABOVE: The gilded flaming urn at the top of the Monument. The Monument, 202 feet high, is a memorial to the Great Fire of London in 1666.

RIGHT, ABOVE: Tower Bridge at sunset.

but the bridge itself lasted until it was replaced by a classical edifice completed in 1831. Somewhat oddly, this second bridge is now to be found in the vicinity of Lake Havasu City, Arizona, whither it was exported in 1967 in favour of a modern concrete span.

Just by the north end of London Bridge and clearly visible from the river there rises a curious, 202-feet high column, once the monarch of the surrounding streets, though now reduced to insignificance by newer giants. This column, invariably referred to simply as 'the Monument', was completed in 1677 to designs by Wren, to commemorate the Great Fire of 1666, which was said to have begun in a baker's shop precisely 202 feet away.

Close by on the waterfront is the Victorian building of Billingsgate, where, until 1982, fish were bought and sold for centuries to the accompaniment of a flow of language from the porters so fluently coarse and extravagantly abusive that from the 17th century at least the name of the place has been synonymous with foul speech. Now the fish market has gone, and the building itself is being converted to other uses. The Worshipful Company of Fishmongers, on the other hand, possess their stately livery hall in great dignity some little way upstream, close by the north end of London Bridge.

Downstream again, sobriety is restored by the grey threat of the Royal Navy's last heavy cruiser, HMS *Belfast*, now moored in her retirement off Symon's Wharf. She was the headquarters ship for the Normandy landings from 6 June 1944 onwards and bombarded the coast as commandos went ashore. Those guns may seem puny if we think of modern missile warfare, but the stacked turrets still carry an aura of power, a hint of naval might past and gone.

Vastly more dated, yet somehow also more intimidating, are the fortifications of the ancient royal stronghold which crouches on the north bank opposite HMS *Belfast*. The Tower of London has always been a fortress, an arsenal and a prison rather than a palace in which kings kept court, and its character shows clearly still in its frowning walls and heavily-protected gates. Long after other castles have been modified for dignity or comfort, handed away to other uses or simply demolished, the Tower continues patiently in its accustomed role. The Crown Jewels are still kept there, and soldiers are quartered in the barracks; the last State Prisoner was

Rudolf Hess, Hitler's Deputy Fuhrer; the circuit of the walls is still intact, and the gates are securely locked each night during the age-old Ceremony of the Keys.

The central strongpoint of the fortress, and the feature that gives it its name, is the massive Norman keep built for William the Conqueror between c.1078 and 1097, to hold down his newly-acquired City of London. Henry III and Edward I added the outer circuits of walls and towers. As a specimen of medieval military architecture it is fascinating; the collections of arms and armour which it houses — not to mention the regalia displayed in the Jewel House — are priceless; the inhabitants, whether Guardsmen, Yeomen Warders or ravens, are colourful and picturesque; but in the end it is the fearful tale of imprisonment and torture, murder and execution, which has stained the Tower's stones over the centuries, that draws the visitors and appals the imagination. This is the darker side of our story of royalty, and as the boat slides past Traitors' Gate it is hard to repress a shudder at the thought of those who passed that way in days gone by.

Coupled with the Tower in the tourist's memory is the striking silhouette of Tower Bridge, as much a symbol of London as is the Eiffel Tower of Paris — and even younger, since it dates from 1886 to 1894. Its 1,000 ton bascules are lifted comparatively rarely nowadays, for the big ships no longer come to the Pool of London, and the original hydraulic machinery — a marvel of its time, capable of opening the channel in under two minutes — has been replaced by an electrical system.

Until a comparatively short while ago, ships passing downstream through Tower Bridge entered the great complex known as the Port of London, and had to thread their way through a throng of ships and barges which crowded the river and filled the huge dock systems which opened off either bank. In recent years, however, the river-trade has moved further downstream — as it has been doing, in fact, for hundreds of years. The medieval quays such as the Queenhythe, mentioned in a charter of Alfred the Great (themselves often incorporating piling from earlier Roman wharfs), lined the north bank above the Tower. In 1696 the first artificial dock, the Great Howland Dock, was built on the south bank at Deptford. Then in the 19th century a succession of new docks extended the port even further downstream.

ABOVE: A Tower Raven. There are six ravens on the establishment at the Tower and two further ravens are allowed as guests. Each one has his or her own personality but will be posted elsewhere if their conduct is unsatisfactory!

ENTRY TO THE TRAITORS' GATE

LEFT: The Tower of London. For 900 years it has been at different times a fortress, a palace and a prison. The famous Traitors' Gate can be seen on the left.

RIGHT: Chief Yeoman Warder in state dress. The 'blue undress' uniform normally worn by Yeomen Warders was designed in Victorian times as the state dress was too expensive to be worn every day.

RIGHT: Tower Bridge, erected in 1894, has become one of the most distinctive landmarks along the course of the river. Each of the twin drawbridges weighs about 1,000 tons and can be raised very quickly to allow large craft to pass underneath.

St Katharine Dock

The St Katharine Dock enjoys a special distinction, as having pioneered new development on London's river twice in its lifetime. When it was first constructed, by the great civil engineer Thomas Telford, in the early years of the 19th century, it inaugurated a whole new era in the history of the Port, by taking ships out of the stream through lock-gates into an enclosed basin, thus enabling them to discharge their cargoes into the safety of warehouses alongside the quays. Over the next hundred years, a whole series of such docks, with ever-roomier basins, more massive lock-gates, vaster warehouses and loftier cranes, was created along both banks of the Thames in imitation of the St Katharine Dock. Meanwhile, she, the original, prospered on the trade of Africa and the East, her warehouses stuffed with spice of the Indies and teas of China.

LEFT: St Katharine Dock and Wapping, showing the extensive redevelopment below Tower Bridge.

LEFT, BELOW: St Katharine Dock, opened in 1808, now transformed into a lively business and tourist centre.

RIGHT: A nostalgic sight of traditional Thames sailing barges with visiting square-rigged training ships.

BELOW: The yacht haven at St Katharine Dock.

When the square-rigged clipper ships ceased to sail, however, the St Katharine Dock was too small to accommodate steamers, and decline set in. The buildings were partially ruined by bombs and fire, and total destruction seemed to be looming when in 1969 the bold decision was taken to renovate the site in something close to its original form, for the new requirements and opportunities of the late 20th century. The surviving warehouses were converted into busy offices and sought-after flats; a new, 826-bed hotel − the Tower Hotel − began attracting a stream of visitors to its incomparable site beside Tower Bridge; and, in 1972, the building of the World Trade Centre re-established St Katharine Dock as the focus of London's commercial activity.

Meanwhile, the basins came to be crowded again with craft, some of them historic vessels such as Thames sailing barges and the old Nore light vessel, others modern luxury yachts and cruisers. Along the quays, boat owners mingle with admiring visitors, and throng the restaurants and pubs which do a roaring trade all through the year. The whole redevelopment demonstrates brilliantly that old urban and commercial sites can be put to effective and desirable modern use without any loss of their identity, and, perhaps still more important, has done much to remind architects, planners, and the general public of the value of water as a component in the urban scene.

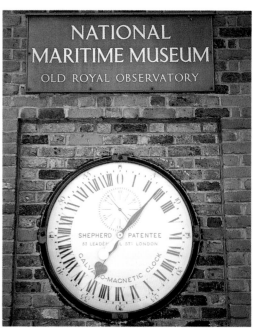

Five miles downstream from London Bridge, on the south bank of the Thames, stands Greenwich; in all England there can be few spots richer in the combination of royal with maritime history. Royal builders were active here from the beginning of the 15th century, and in 1427 Humphrey, Duke of Gloucester, enclosed a park and erected a watchtower on the site later occupied by the Royal Observatory. The original royal palace known as Placentia, or the Pleasaunce, has long since gone, but Henry VIII, Mary I and Elizabeth I were all born there, and they and their Stuart successors often went there to enjoy the pleasures of a country retreat, while remaining close to the centre of power. Sir Walter Raleigh came too — here at Greenwich he is supposed to have laid his cloak across a muddy path before Elizabeth's feet.

But the palmiest days for Greenwich came in the 17th century. In 1616 Inigo Jones was commissioned to build a house for James I's queen, Anne of Denmark; now known simply as the Queen's House, it is regarded as one of the most important, and perfect, early classical buildings in England. Later in the century, Charles II began to build a palace for himself, which in turn was incorporated after 1694 in Wren's much grander design for a Royal Hospital for seamen, comparable to that established at Chelsea for soldiers. Hawksmoor and Vanbrugh were also associated with the work, which was not fully

ABOVE: The *Cutty Sark* in dry dock beside the Royal Naval College at Greenwich. This famous clipper carried wool, tea, redwood and sugar from Australia and could sail over 1,000 miles in three days.

RIGHT: The Royal Naval College, one of Wren's great masterpieces, presents an unforgettable vista across the river.

FAR RIGHT: The 24-hour Magnetic Clock built into the wall outside the gates of the Old Royal Observatory, now part of the National Maritime Museum.

RIGHT: The traditional buildings of maritime Greenwich contrast with the new Docklands developments in the Isle of Dogs beyond. The Royal Observatory (in the foreground) stands on the Greenwich meridian 'dividing' East from West.

BELOW: *Gipsy Moth IV,* the tiny yacht in which Sir Francis Chichester circumnavigated the globe single-handed in 1966-67.

completed until 1745. The result has been called 'the most stately procession of buildings we possess ... one of the most sublime sights English architecture affords ... where no careless or muddled efforts exist, where, indeed, no mean ideas can live'. In 1873 the Hospital became the Royal Naval College; the Queen's House, much restored, is now part of the National Maritime Museum; and the Old Royal Observatory, also part of the museum, has been returned to its original 17th-century state.

The National Maritime Museum possesses an unrivalled collection of models, pictures, and every sort of relic from Britain's naval past, and its huge wealth of resources enables it to mount a constantly changing series of special exhibitions, often incorporating imaginative reconstructions of scenes and episodes from the days of sail.

Two famous sailing vessels lie in dry dock near the National Maritime Museum — the Queen of the China tea-clippers, *Cutty Sark,* and the yacht in which Sir Francis Chichester achieved his epic single-handed circum-

navigation of the globe, *Gipsy Moth IV.* They are, in fact, the last of a long sequence of picturesque and impressive vessels which have come in their retirement to line the banks of the Thames between Westminster and Greenwich; some, such as the paddle-steamer *Tattershall Castle,* and the sailing barge *Wilfred,* along the Victoria Embankment, serve as restaurants or wine bars, while others, such as the schooner *Kathleen and Mary* near Southwark Cathedral, are owned and exhibited by the Maritime Trust. All of them serve as reminders that we are in a city with a great maritime history.

Less easy to visit are the buildings of the Royal Naval College. If the chance offers to see the Painted Hall which is the centrepiece of Wren's great scheme, however, it should not be missed. The serene majesty of its architecture, and the breath-taking splendour of its decoration, make it one of the most wonderful rooms in the world; the young naval officer who is privileged to dine here must know, beyond a doubt, that he is the inheritor of a matchless tradition.

The story of London's Royal River is one of constant change: the ebb and flow of prosperity, the rise and fall of monarchs and merchants, have left their marks on its banks over the centuries. It is peculiarly apt that the last stage in our journey towards the sea should take us to the newest, and some would say the most remarkable, of the innumerable building projects which have loaded the patient riverside soil — Docklands.

During the 19th century, the north bank of the Thames beyond the Tower was progressively excavated into a whole series of artificial lakes, as ever-larger docks were created to serve the ever-larger merchant vessels. The West India and Millwall Docks, the Royal Victoria, the Royal Albert, and finally the King George V Docks, in their heyday sheltered hundreds of thousands of tons of merchant shipping, loading the exports of Britain when she was the workshop of the world, and disgorging from their returning holds the wealth of a global empire.

Since the war, however, in a change more rapid than any previous development in the

LEFT: A pilot's-eye view of London City Airport, opened in 1987. Designed for short take-off and landing aircraft, it is a convenient alternative to London's major airports.

BELOW LEFT: The ultra-modern Docklands Light Railway links the massive developments in Docklands with the City.

ABOVE: New waterside offices and marina in Docklands. Development around the abandoned and obsolete docks has been ceaseless since the early 1970s and imaginative new buildings for every purpose have been, and still are being, created.

ABOVE RIGHT: An evening view of the river at Wapping.

history of the Port of London, all these docks, so painstakingly created, have been abandoned in favour of a huge new development at Tilbury, 25 miles below London Bridge. There, the new container ships are stacked and unstacked with a speed and ease unheard of in the days when sweating stevedores hauled sacks and bales and crates from the holds of tramp steamers. This left 2,000 acres lying virtually idle, on the doorstep of one of the world's most crowded cities.

Following the successful redevelopment of the St Katharine Dock in the early 1970s, the developers' eyes moved on to the empty expanses downstream. What has happened since then, and is still happening, is one of the most dramatic stories of urban renewal ever seen, in Britain or elsewhere.

Huge buildings, in every style and for every purpose, are sprouting on all sides, amid the ruined relics of older uses and the stagnant pools of abandoned docks. Construction never seems to cease, and properties are frenziedly bought and sold several times over before they are even ready for occupation. Following the example of the St Katharine Dock scheme, the old basins are being given positive value, both as elements in the landscape and as economically functioning utilities such as marinas; but it is the land property that has attracted the speculators.

For an area so vast, almost a new town on its own, the creation of fresh systems of communication was an early and pressing priority. The river itself has met part of the need — there can be no better, or easier way to travel from, say, the Isle of Dogs to work in the City or Whitehall, than by scudding up the river in a fast launch. The riverbus service plies continuously between Docklands and Chelsea Harbour, at 15-minute intervals.

A second feature of the Docklands' transportation scene — the Docklands Light Railway — uses the latest computer-aided technology. This brilliantly ingenious system whisks passengers with smooth speed from the squat turret that marks the entrance to the Greenwich footway tunnel into the very heart of the City. Its gaily coloured, cheerfully futuristic station buildings and elegantly curving overhead lines catch the spirit of mingled enterprise and optimism that characterised the first railway developments in the mid-19th century.

Finally, the longer-distance needs of Docklands are met by the London City Airport which was opened in 1987 for use by aircraft specially designed for short take-off and landing. It seems certain to feature large in the Docklands' scheme of things to come.

The Thames Barrier

In contrast to the classical splendours of Greenwich, a short distance down river lies the new Thames Barrier, constructed to protect London from the risk of flooding. This magnificent feat of modern engineering was officially opened by the Queen in 1984, and completed in 1987. Like others of Europe's great maritime cities, London is gradually sinking below the level of the neighbouring waters. Now, however, the banks are safer from flooding than they have been for decades, and the stream eddies round yet another monument to London's constantly changing relationship with its majestic river.

ABOVE: Completed in 1987, the Thames Barrier consists of a series of movable gates built side-by-side across the river, to protect London from flooding.

ABOVE: A view of the Thames Barrier by night.

ACKNOWLEDGEMENTS
Illustrations are reproduced by kind permission of the following: British Tourist Authority: 10 (above left and right), 20 (above). Chorley & Handford: 26 (above). Robert Harding Picture Library: 6 (above right), 8 (below), 21 (below), 23 (below), 26 (below), 27 (left). Angelo Hornak: 14 (below). Images Colour Library: front cover, 13 (above), 28-29. A.F. Kersting 6 (below), 7 (below), 9 (below). Andrew Lawson: 10 (below right), 24 (below left). London Aerial Photo Library: 22 (above). National Maritime Museum: 25 (above). The Photo Source: 9 (above), 13 (below), 15 (above), 17 (main picture), 18 (above). PictureBank Photo Library: back cover, 5 (above), 10 (below left), 12,15 (below), 19 (left), 20 (below), 22 (below), 24 (below right), 28 (left). Picturepoint: 5 (below), 7 (above right). Property Services Agency (Crown copyright): 4. Mike Roberts: 2,3 (above right and below). Kenneth Scowen, FIIP. FRPS: 8 (above), 11, 14 (above right). Brian Shuel: 17 (inset), 23 (above). Tony Stone Photolibrary – London: 6 (above left), 21 (above). Vision International: 19 (right), 27 (right). Visionbank Library and England Scene: 7 (above left). Andy Williams: 18 (below). ZEFA: 14 (above left). The photographs on pages 3 (above left), 24 (above) and 25 (below) are copyright Pitkin Pictorials.

Designed by Crispin Goodall.
Map by Mark Richards.
Picture research by Ann Lockhart.

First published by Pitkin Pictorials Ltd, 1982.
This edition © Pitkin Pictorials 1989.

Typeset by the Ikthos Studios, Andover, Hampshire.
Printed in Great Britain by ABC Printers, Ditchling, Sussex.

ISBN 0 85372 460 1

FRONT COVER: Fireworks cascade over Tower Bridge.

BACK COVER: Hampton Court Palace: view from the river.

For London tourist information, contact THE TOURIST INFORMATION CENTRE VICTORIA STATION (Tel: 01 730 3488).

189/30